INVENTORS

HENRY FORD

PAUL JOSEPH
ABDO & Daughters

Published by Abdo & Daughters, 4940 Viking Drive, Suite 622, Edina, Minnesota 55435.

Printed in the United States.

Cover illustration and icon: Kristen Copham
Interior photos: Bettmann, pages 15, 22, 24
      Wide World Photos, pages 5, 7, 9, 11, 17, 28
      Archive Photos, page 12
Photo colorization: Professional Litho

Edited by Bob Italia

Library of Congress Cataloging-in-Publication Data

Joseph, Paul, 1970-
Henry Ford / Paul Joseph.
  p. cm. — (Inventors)
Includes index.
Summary: Sketches the life of the inventor and businessman who with hard work and an innovative mind changed the car industry in ways that will never be duplicated.
ISBN 1-56239-636-6
1. Ford, Henry, 1863-1947—Juvenile literature. 2. Automobile industry and trade—United States—History—Juvenile literature. 3. Businessmen—United States—Biography—Juvenile literature. [1. Ford, Henry, 1863-1947. 2. Automobile industry and trade—Biography. 3. Businessmen.] I. Title. II. Series: Inventors (Series)
HD9710.U52F6643 1996
338.7'6292'092—dc20
[B]   95-51269
              CIP
              AC

Contents

Henry

Although many people believe that Henry Ford invented the **automobile,** that honor goes to German inventor Karl Benz. But what Henry did for the automobile industry will be remembered forever.

Ford's greatest invention was the Model T car. The Model T was a huge success in the United States because they were affordable to working class people of America. Ford used his **assembly line** to make car production fast and inexpensive.

Ford also formed a credit company to loan people money to buy cars. People would repay the loan in small monthly payments with **interest**. This remains the most popular way to buy cars.

Henry Ford changed the car industry in ways that will never be matched. He did it with hard work and an **innovative** mind.

Henry Ford in later years sitting in one of his original automobiles.

The Early Years

Henry Ford was born on July 30, 1863. He spent his early years in Dearborn, Michigan, working on his family's farm. He didn't like farm work because he found it boring.

With his spare time, Henry tinkered in the farm's **blacksmith shop**. He wanted to design and build machines. He was certain that someday machines would take the place of horse-drawn wagons and plows.

Henry was a good student. His favorite subject was math, in which he excelled. His arithmetic skills helped him later in life with car designs.

Henry Ford as a young child.

His First Jobs

Henry decided to leave the family farm at age 17. He wanted to learn more about many different things. So he moved to Detroit and found a job at the Flower Machine Shop. The shop made large brass and iron parts such as valves and fire hydrants. Henry grew tired of the work and quit after nine months.

Henry's next job was one that he loved and gave him very valuable experience. He worked at Detroit Drydock Company, a business that built steamship **engines**.

Henry became a certified machinist in 1882. Westinghouse Company hired him to travel around Michigan to set up and repair steam engines. Henry continued to think about a better way to build a lighter, more powerful engine.

The employees of the Edison Illumination Company. Henry Ford is in the top row, third from the right.

In 1888, Henry married Clara Bryant. During his spare time, he worked on a lightweight engine in his workshop. By 1891, Henry designed a small engine that burned gasoline.

Because of Henry's knowledge of engines, Thomas Edison offered him the chief engineer job for Edison Illuminating Company. Henry ran the **generators** that supplied **electricity** to Edison's customers. In 1893, the Ford's celebrated the birth of their son, Edsel.

His First Cars

In 1894, Henry finally built his gasoline-powered car. He mounted the **engine** on a four-wheel carriage, hopped onto the carriage, and drove it. His neighbors looked on in amazement. He called it the "horseless carriage" and began selling them.

Henry wanted to make cars full time, so he quit his job at Edison Illuminating. Now he wanted to design a quieter, sturdier engine.

By June 1903, Henry owned a small manufacturing plant in Detroit called the Ford Motor Company. He hired 10 workers to **assemble** cars.

FIRST · CAR

The man who put the world on wheels, Henry Ford, with his first car, built in 1896.

The Model A, built in 1903.

The first **automobile** rolled out that month. It was called the Model A. It had two forward speeds, a reverse gear, and a top speed of 30 miles (48 km) per hour. Each car cost $850. By the next month, Ford was making 15 cars a day.

The first year, Henry worked many long hours. Often he would help his workers. His hard work paid off. By 1905, business had become so good that Ford had outgrown its factory. The company constructed a building which was 10 times larger than the original factory. Henry was on his way to becoming the most famous car manufacturer in the world.

The Model T

    With the success of the Model A, Henry knew that people wanted cars. So he began looking to the future. He decided to build an inexpensive car that everyone could afford.

    "The way to make **automobiles** is to make one automobile like another automobile," Henry said, "to make them all alike, to make them come through the factory all alike. If you freeze the design and concentrate on production, as the volume goes up, the cars are certain to become cheaper. I want to turn out a car that the workingman can buy."

    Henry called this car the Model T. The Model T was introduced in 1908. It would forever change the face of the nation. A hood covered the front **engine**. Its four **cylinders** could produce a top speed of 45 mph, and it got 20 miles per gallon of gas.

The pride of the Ford Motor Company: The Model T.

The Model T was so successful that Ford needed a much bigger factory. Henry decided to build the largest car factory in the world.

The factory was built of concrete, steel, and had more than 50,000 square feet (15,240 square meters) of windows. The new factory was known as the Crystal Palace. Ford moved into the factory in 1910.

The Assembly Line

In the new factory, the workers made the Model T on an **assembly line**, which made production fast and inexpensive. This concept **revolutionized** car manufacturing, and made buying a car much easier for the average American.

Ford made the Model A in the traditional way. Workers made each car at its own spot on the factory floor. Workers had to carry parts to each assembly spot to build cars.

On the assembly line, the Model T moved while the workers stayed in one place. Each worker fitted one part to the car. As the Model T moved past the line of workers, the car was built part by part.

Opposite page: Model T Fords ready for delivery after leaving the assembly line.

Henry Ford's

1863*
Born
July 30
Dearborn, MI.

1880*
Works
at Flower
Machine Shop,
Detroit.

1882
Becomes
certified
Machinist.

1888
Ford
marries
Clara Bryant.

1908
The Model
T is intro-
duced.

1910
Opens a new
factory called
Crystal Palace.

1913
Ford
sells
200,000
cars in
one year.

1917
Ford
makes war
equipment.

**Detail
Area**

1945
Grandson
Henry Ford II
becomes
President of
the Ford Motor
Company.

Life & Invention Timeline

1891
Designs small engine to run on gasoline.

1892
Ford becomes Chief Engineer for Edison Illuminating Co.

1894
Constructs an engine that runs on gasoline.

1903
Opens the Ford Motor Co. The Model A is introduced.

1924
Ford sells his 10 millionth Model T.

1927
Introduces the new Model A.

1932
The Ford V-8 is introduced.

1941
Ford builds tanks, trucks, and other war equipment.

1947
Dies April, 7th.

With the **assembly line**, production time for each car dropped from 12.5 hours to 2 hours and 38 minutes. By 1913, Ford was selling 200,000 cars per year. By January 1914, Ford was making a Model T every 93 minutes.

Henry did not invent the assembly line. But he used it well—and became an American hero. Now, almost everyone could afford a car.

In 1924, Henry sold his 10 millionth Model T. But suddenly, in 1925, sales of the Model T began to decline. The Model T was not keeping up with the competition, which featured a self-starter that started the engine with the turn of a key, and removable tires.

The New Model A

Henry had difficulty changing the car that had made him rich and famous. He insisted on producing more Model T's. But the sales continued to fall.

The Ford Motor Company announced on May 25, 1927, that it would build a new car. It was called the new Model A. At the announcement, Henry said good-bye to the Model T.

"The Model T was a **pioneer**," he stated to a crowd of reporters. "Things are changing. A newer car is needed. But the Model T will always hold a place in American history for its contributions. It was the car that ran before there were good roads to run on. It broke down the barriers by bringing people closer together. We are still proud of the Model T Ford."

Henry Ford (left) rides in the last Model T ever made.

The next day, Henry rode the 15 millionth—and last—Model T from the factory. Then the company shut down the Model T **assembly line** for good.

The first new Model A rolled off the assembly line in October 1927. Several were introduced at car dealers on December 1, 1927. Everyone loved it. Soon, the public was buying thousands.

The new Model A was more modern than the Model T. It had a quieter, more powerful four-**cylinder engine** that could go 65 miles (105 km) per hour. It also had an ignition system that started the car with the turn of a key. There was even a safety-glass windshield that was difficult to shatter.

The new Model A was a great success. By the end of 1928, Ford was producing 6,400 cars per day. In 1929, the company made nearly two million cars.

Ford Weathers the Storm

Henry wanted everyone to have a Model A. So he introduced a way for people to buy a car through his finance company, the Universal Credit Company. Ford lent money to the buyer who would repay the loan in small monthly amounts. Almost everyone who bought a Model A borrowed money from Universal. It is still the most popular way to buy a car today.

On October 29, 1929, the **stock market** crashed. This caused a huge panic across America. People rushed to their banks to take out their money. But most banks did not have enough

Opposite page: The successor of the Model T, the new Model A.

money to cover all the withdrawls. Many banks went out of business. Millions of people lost their savings. With no money to spend, many businesses failed. Now people had no money or jobs. The **Great Depression** had begun.

At first, the **stock market** crash did not affect Ford. Henry did not lose his money. In fact, he had enough cash to give his employees raises. But by 1931, car sales declined. The company lost money and had its worst year.

Henry knew how to weather the storm. He built a new car called the Ford V-8. It had an eight-**cylinder engine**, a new **transmission**, and only cost $460.

The V-8 sold very well. By 1934, Ford Motor Company was making money again.

Making a Difference

On December 7, 1941, the Japanese attacked Pearl Harbor in Honolulu, Hawaii. Suddenly, the United States was involved in World War II, which Germany had started in Europe in 1939. The United States needed many tanks, trucks, and bombers to fight Germany and Japan.

Henry stopped producing cars and began making war equipment. He even built a new factory near Detroit. Eventually, Ford made 650 bombers per month.

In 1943, tragedy struck when Edsel Ford died of cancer. Even more, Henry's health was failing. He could not continue as head of his company. His grandson, Henry Ford II, returned from the navy and took over for his grandfather.

Inventor Henry Ford.

Henry was happy with his grandson. Henry II worked very hard, and helped the company run better. Ford's future was secure.

Henry turned his full attention to the Ford Foundation. This organization gave money to schools, museums, hospitals, and other worthy causes.

On April 7, 1947, Henry died of a stroke at the age of 84. He left most of his fortune to the Ford Foundation, making it one of the largest in America.

Henry Ford will always be remembered as an **innovative** man who made the automobile affordable—and changed the face of the world.

Glossary

assemble (uh-SEM-bull) - To put something together.

assembly line - An arrangement of machines and people where work passes from person to person in a direct line until the work is complete.

automobile (awe-toe-moe-BEE-ull) - A four-wheeled vehicle made to take people to their destination.

blacksmith shop - Where tools and horseshoes are made and repaired.

cylinder (SILL-un-der) - The part of a car engine that contains a piston.

electricity (e-leck-TRISS-uh-tee) - A current or power.

engine (EN-jin)- A piece of equipment that has power to make things go such as a car or ship.

generator (JEN-er-ay-tore) - A machine that changes energy into electrical energy.

Great Depression (dee-PRESH-un) - A time in the United States when the stock market crashed and many people were out of work and didn't have money.

ignition (ig-NISH-un) - The switch in a gasoline engine.

innovative (in-no-VAY-tiv) - To come up with ideas and do things in a new way, a way that has never been done before.

interest (IN-trest) - The money paid for use of someone else's money.

Model T - One of the first cars made in the United States and also one of the most popular.

pioneer (pie-oh-NEAR) - A person that is the first to do something in a particular field.

revolutionize (rev-oh-LEW-shun-eyes) - To make huge changes for the better.

stock market - A market for stocks in the country.

transmission (trans-MISH-un) - The part of a car that transmits power from the engine to the front or rear axle by the use of gears.

Index

921
FOR   Joseph, Paul.

Henry Ford

DATE DUE	BORROWER'S NAME	ROOM NUMBER

DATE DUE

921
FOR   Joseph, Paul.

Henry Ford